Contents

A MACDONALD BOOK

© Hachette, Paris, 1986

First published in France in 1986 by
Hachette Jeunesse
as *Animaux des Rivières et des Etangs*

First published in Great Britain in 1987 by
Macdonald & Company (Publishers) Ltd
London & Sydney
A BPCC plc company

Printed and bound in France

Macdonald & Company (Publishers) Ltd
Greater London House
Hampstead Road
London NW1 7QX

Credits
This edition produced for Macdonald Publishers by
Lionheart Books,
10 Chelmsford Square, London NW10 3AR.

Translated by Madeleine Bender
Adapted by Lionel Bender
Artwork services by Radius

British Library Cataloguing in Publication Data
Bender, Lionel
   Rivers and ponds.—(Nature notes; 4)
   1. Stream fauna—Europe—Juvenile
literature 2. Pond fauna—Europe—
Juvenile literature
   I. Title II. Bender, Madeleine III. Series
591.94   QL253

ISBN 0-356-11992-0

RIVERS AND PONDS

Translated by Madeleine Bender
Adapted by Lionel Bender

Throughout the world, most areas have rivers flowing through them or are dotted with lakes or ponds. Fresh water is the source of all life forms and people have always settled close to it since it satisfies both our drinking needs and the requirements of agriculture and industry for water.

Rivers and ponds are full of surprises for the inquisitive naturalist. But you must take time to observe and study. Very often you will find that a simple magnifying glass or a pair of binoculars are your most precious tools for watching freshwater creatures. Sometimes a fishing rod will be particularly useful and it is worthwhile making a little fine fishing net to collect specimens.

Whenever you are examining a river or a pond, be careful not to upset the environment. Put back branches and stones you have touched. Watch birds from a distance so as not to frighten them. If you have to capture an animal to study it, take care you do not harm it. When you have finished your study, put the animal back where you found it.

The Common Heron

A SOCIABLE AND SOLITARY ANIMAL

It is a wader, perched on stilt-like legs. Its very long toes help it to walk easily in mud. It stands poised by the water, its S-shaped neck like a coiled spring. Suddenly it thrusts out its long dagger-shaped yellow bill at its prey.

The common heron is grey with long black feathers on the back. The cheeks, face and neck are lighter, almost white. The back of the head is adorned with a crest. This bird is not very vocal. It has a short but raucous and loud call. It is not a good flyer but it has great stamina. It can travel more than 1000 kilometres during its migrations.

In the breeding season, the heron lives in colonies, or heronries, established in large trees such as poplars or sallows some distance from the hunting grounds.

The nest is a large but simple structure of sticks and twigs. The male and female build it together in the top of a tree or, more rarely, in reeds at the water's edge. In it, the female lays four or five light-green eggs, which are incubated for four weeks.

In contrast, when searching for food at lakesides, ponds or reed-beds, the heron leads a solitary life.

A DAY'S FISHING

If you happen to see a heron by the side of a pond, you can easily observe its habits provided you are as patient as it is. The bird stalks its prey, its harpoon-like bill at the ready.

Your long wait is at last rewarded. The heron goes slowly into the shallow water. It walks quietly, lifting its feet carefully, its neck craned. Hardly has it caught a glimpse of the prey that it shoots its head forward and thrusts its sharp bill at the target with lightning speed and deadly accuracy.

It attacks and eats its various prey in different ways. It plucks small fish from a depth of about ten centimetres, throws them up in the air so that they come down head-first into its bill and swallows them whole. With a larger fish, such as a tench or eel, it throws its prey to the ground to stun it then gobbles it up.

Its hunger satisfied, the heron flies back to the heronry with slow and heavy wing beats.

AN EVIL-SMELLING COLONY

Large heronries are rare and often difficult to get close to. If you are lucky enough to know of one not far from your pond, you can make many fascinating observations. But first get permission to visit the site from the owner of the land and go along with an experienced birdwatcher. Position yourself far enough away so as not to disturb the birds and look through your binoculars.

The parents feed the baby herons with regurgitated food, that is food that has been partly digested and brought back up into the bill. Sometimes the chicks pull on their parents' bill – they want to be served more quickly!

In autumn, when the birds have left the colony, the remains of the herons' meals can be found on the ground or in the water. They include bones, fish bones, hairs, the elytra of beetles, all of which have been regurgitated in pellet form. The pellets lie among excrement,

The heron stands in the water and waits for its prey. It catches it, then swallows it.

pieces of eggs and corpses of young herons fallen from the nests.

THE HERON KEEPS THE BALANCE

The heron is a surface fisher and does not threaten fish such as carp that live in deep water. Also, it only takes the amount of food that it needs and spreads its catches over several species. Do not take notice, therefore, of people who may try to persuade you that the heron is a pest and causes great damage to pond and river life.

The common heron rids us of rodents and insects, which make up two-thirds of its food. It plays a part in regulating the fish population. It preys first on weak or sick fish and, in that way, limits the spread of fish diseases in freshwater habitats. The heron's leftovers, when they fall in the water, encourage the growth of plankton, upon which all the other aquatic creatures eventually depend for their food.

DRY-CLEANING THE FEATHERS

All herons and their relatives have one thing in common: powder down patches. Herons have three such patches, one on the breast and one behind each thigh. They are small areas of downy feathers that crumble into fine powder when rubbed. The herons work the powder into their plumage with their bill then comb it out with their serrated middle claws, cleaning off the slime collected in their feathers after feeding on fish.

THE PURPLE HERON

Less numerous than the common heron but living in the same habitat is the purple heron, which has reddish-brown plumage.

Like the common heron, it nests in colonies, and the two species are sometimes found feeding together on the same marshes.

Keeping away so as not to disturb the birds, you can observe a herons' nest.

The Diving Beetle

A diving beetle larva.

A VORACIOUS INSECT

Large and dark, completely smooth, with a golden yellow band round the edges of the thorax and wing covers, the diving beetle lives in water but can fly if the need arises. When the beetle is about to fly, the 'shell' splits down the middle and the protective wing cases, or elytra, open to allow the thin and transparent wings to spread out.

The adult diving beetle catches its prey with its legs and tears it to shreds with its powerful mandibles. Only those insects with an armour-like 'shell' can escape it. It devours anything edible and when everything has gone from its present territory, it flies off to another puddle or pond.

The diving beetle does not breathe under water. It dives with its own air reserve, stored under its elytra, just like a diver carries oxygen bottles on his back. It comes back to the surface at regular intervals and allows the back of its wing cases to come out of the water to fill up with fresh air. To stay under water, the beetle has to keep moving; if it stops, it automatically rises to the surface just like a cork.

It is the fastest of the pond insects. It swims using mainly its flat, broad hindlegs, which act like paddles. Its oval shape, making it look like an upside-down rowing boat, allows it to glide swiftly through vegetation.

AT THE EDGE OF THE POND

The pond at the bottom of the meadow is an ideal place to observe the diving beetle in action.

Go up close to the pond without making noise and sit down at the edge.

11

Look carefully at the seemingly still water. Soon you will notice an extraordinary amount of activity. Countless animals are moving about in the water, some swimming, others floating. To study these more closely, you will need to collect a small sample of pond life.

A COLLECTING NET

You can use an ordinary fishing net to catch pond creatures but it is simple enough to make your own collecting net. All you require is a forked branch, a piece of sackcloth and some wire to bind the cloth to the branch. The finer the mesh of the cloth the smaller the animals you will be able to collect. Explore the pond with this net and sort through what you have gathered.

With its plants and animals, the pond is a very fragile environment. However, you will not upset the balance of nature if you follow these two rules:

Remove from the pond only the creatures that you want to study.

Unless there are many in the pond keep your captured animals for only a few days then return them to the pond.

You may be lucky and catch the larva of a diving beetle. You can take this in your hand, it is not dangerous. Put it in your collecting jar or bucket. It will settle just below the surface of the water, head down, with its two feathery tail-tips poking up a little into the air to allow it to breathe. It will remain motionless.

THE AQUARIUM

You can keep the diving beetle larva for a day or two in an aquarium or a

At regular intervals, the adult diving beetle comes to the surface to collect air.

The common grey heron is one of the animals that prey on the adult diving beetle.

glass jar. If you are going to put an adult beetle into the aquarium as well, you will need to put fine wiremesh or a piece of loosely woven cloth over the top to prevent the insect flying away. Feed your larva a tadpole and watch the massacre that follows. The larva springs on its prey, seizes it, and digs in its calliper-like mandibles. Quickly it injects into the tadpole digestive juices that paralyse the animal and change its flesh into a 'soup'. The beetle larva then sucks up the liquefied insides of the tadpole leaving only its skin.

A FEW SIMPLE PRECAUTIONS

To keep your larva for any length of time, fill the aquarium with pond or stream water. Tap water contains chlorine which will kill it.

In the aquarium, place some plants. During the day, the plants will absorb the carbon dioxide given out by the animals and produce oxygen. If your 'gas works' work properly, you won't need to change the water for some time.

In a separate bucket of pond water, keep a stock of prey for your larva: tadpoles, leeches, worms, small fish. Regularly you will have to remove the insect cases and other left-overs of your 'pet's' meals since they will poison the water as they decompose.

THE BEETLE FAMILY

The diving beetle is one of many insects within the Coleoptera or beetle family. They all have elytra, the hard wing cases that protect the folded back flying wings when the animal is at rest. Ladybirds, the Colorado beetle, cockchafers, carabid beetles are all Coleoptera.

The European Beaver

AN ANIMAL OF BYGONE DAYS

Recalled in place and river names in areas it used to visit – for example Beverley, meaning beaver stream, is the name of a town in Humberside – the beaver was very common in the Middle Ages. Its pelt was used to make hats and its flesh was cooked and eaten.

In the 16th and 17th centuries, castoreum, a secretion from a gland under the animal's tail, was thought to have incredible healing qualities. Scientists have since found that castoreum contains salicylic acid, one of the ingredients of aspirin. Beavers use castoreum, with its characteristic smell, to mark the boundaries of their territory. Each beaver family controls a three- to five-kilometre stretch of river and will chase off any strange beaver.

There are no longer any beavers in Britain but they still live in Scandinavia, Germany, France, European Russia.

LIFE BY THE WATER'S EDGE

The beaver is the largest of the European rodents. It has small rounded ears, a stout body that makes it look heavy, and its fur can be almost any shade of brown. It can only live near water and never moves away from it by more than about thirty metres. It feeds only on plant material, which it collects from under water and on the banks. Like all rodents it has powerful incisor teeth. In between the incisors and the molar teeth instead of canine teeth there is a gap that enables the animal to hold and carry thick branches in its jaw.

The front paws have five free toes each armed with a sharp claw that the beaver uses for digging. The hind paws have webbed toes like those of a duck and two claws used for combing fur. The broad, flat tail is scaly with sharp edges. It is used for swimming and diving. A water-repellent outer covering of sleek, long guard hairs protects the fine downy underfur.

Clumsy on dry land, the beaver is perfectly adapted to aquatic life. Since it emerges from its home during the night-time, it is difficult to observe but it leaves distinctive tracks and signs.

A beaver family is composed of a parent pair that mate for life and their young, which stay with the couple for two years. The female has one litter a year of two or four young. Therefore each burrow houses an average of about ten beavers. Just after the birth of a new litter, at the end of May or beginning of June, the two-year-old beavers leave the family to go and settle elsewhere.

THE REMAINS OF A MEAL

On the river bank, many tree trunks show the beavers' cone-shaped tooth cuts that make them look like the sharpened ends of two pencils joined together.

In winter the beaver feeds by gnawing the bark of willow or black poplar trees. Sometimes it destroys the tops of the trees. The stumps grow new shoots and gradually thick bunches of branches appear. The appearance of the woodland changes under the influence of the animal.

Here and there willow or hazelnut tree shoots have been severed with a neat, slanting cut, like the cut made by a knife. Run your finger across the cut surface. You can feel the slight ridges left by the beaver's sharp incisors. The beaver makes the most of aquatic plants

The female beaver suckles its young for about two months.

The beaver has few natural enemies. It knows how to escape from foxes and other aggressors.

The entrance to the lodge is built under the surface of the water. In this way the beaver protects itself from its enemies and the winter cold.

collected from the bottom of the river and of the herbaceous plants from the banks. At the end of summer, in shallow water, it piles up a collection of sticks and other plant material.

A WISE BUILDER

As you walk by, you give this heap of wood only a casual glance. The heap is, however, a beaver's hut, or lodge, which the animal is repairing. Among the dead wood gathered from the surrounding area there are pieces of live branches cut from trees close by. The beaver carries the heaviest building materials to the lodge between its forelegs and its chin.

The level of some rivers gets lower during dry spells and then the entrance to the lodge becomes visible. To keep the water level constant, the wise

occupants of the lodge construct a fifty-to seventy-five-centimetre high dam across the river using more branches and sticks. The buttresses and supports of these dams are beautifully engineered.

IT WENT THAT WAY

Several paths leading to the river reveal the continuous comings and goings of the beaver to the spots where it gathers wood. In places you may find tunnels dug under low-growing vegetation. In the water you can sometimes see ripples made by the beaver as it swims along. On dry sand, trails left by branches being dragged along signal the animals are busy building their lodge. Note, too, the muddle of pawmarks in the mud.

The Great Crested Grebe

WEDDING SUIT AND TRAVELLING COSTUME

On stretches of water you can identify the great crested grebe by its spectacular and frequent dives, its long, sharp beak and the double black crest on its head. In spring, in its mating plumage, it boasts a superb rust-coloured ruff above its white neck and abdomen. Its back is brown. In autumn, before migration, the crest and the ruff disappear almost completely.

AT HOME IN WATER

As with some other aquatic birds, the grebe's legs are positioned at the back of its body and make it difficult for the animal to walk on land. The grebe does not fly much either and covers long distances only on its migrations in November and March. Rather than true seasonal migrations, these are more searches for water that is not frozen and for breeding sites. Sometimes in winter very large numbers of grebes are found concentrated on small ice-free expanses of water.

Indeed, the bird never travels far away from water. On a pond, lake or reservoir it displays its talents as a swimmer and a diver using its paddle-like feet to push against the water just like a coot.

FEEDING ON FISH AND FEATHERS

It is from the water that it voraciously extracts its food – 200 grams of medium-sized fish a day. Because of this, it was long considered to be a pest. If it brings up grasses in its beak from the lake bed, these are not to eat but are an offering of friendship to its partner.

Strangely, the grebe eats its own bod feathers and feeds them to its young after soaking them. In the bird's stomach the feathers break down to form a sort of felt-like material that is thought to make it easier for the grebe to regurgitate sharp fish bones. Great crested grebes used to be actively hunted for their feathers, which were used to adorn ladies' hats. They are now totally protected.

A FLOATING ISLAND

Ponds are good places for watching birds. Position yourself carefully and you can watch, at the same time, open water, places of concealment such as reedbeds, and the banks. Having found a good site, you can put up a hide and study the birds using binoculars. But you must be careful: pond life is as fragile as it is rich.

Good places to visit are those where bulrushes and reeds grow in large quantities. Go in among the rushes carefully, making sure the path you create does not appear too obvious to the birds. Of course, you must absolutely avoid such areas during the nesting period, from April to July.

You may be lucky and discover, near the edge, a large shapeless heap of plants that is more or less dry on the surface but sodden at the bottom. It is the abandoned nest of the great crested grebe. It floats a little like a raft but more like an iceberg as the greater part of it is under water. It is tied to the reed stalks, giving the impression of a house built on piles. Sometimes, breaking its

The great crested grebe catches its food by diving. It pursues fish under water.

moorings, the nest drifts away. The grebe built it with rotting waterweeds that it found at the bottom of the pond. Imagine the number of trips underwater it must have made to collect enough material. When the nest was complete the female laid four whitish eggs in it.

SURVIVAL OF THE FITTEST

As the chicks grow, so does their appetite. Then it is the strongest ones that get the food from the parents. The weaker ones end up starving to death. What seems like heartless behaviour on the part of the parents is in fact obedience to the law of natural selection: only the fittest survive.

DIVING COMPETITIONS

A grebe you are observing suddenly disappears. It has dived in search of food. A second or two passes then back up it comes. Now it is another's turn to dive. It is a female that is carrying her young on her back. The two passengers slip from their perch into the water and pop back up to the surface straight away like corks; they do not yet know how to dive properly.

Now try this game. Sit down comfortably and take out your watch. If you have brought a notebook and a pencil with you, get ready to write down some figures. Time each dive. Record and compare the performances of each bird. Careful, though: the birds do not always reappear where you expect them to. With a friend you can play guessing games, choosing when and where each bird will surface and what it brings back in its beak.

A little way off something looking like a periscope is moving slowly along the edge of the reeds. It is the head of a great crested grebe. Disturbed by a noisy passer-by, the bird uses the same technique as a submarine for searching the surface of the water without being seen. By flattening its feathers against its body, it squeezes out the air trapped between them. This makes it less buoyant and its body becomes half submerged in the water; only its head shows above the surface.

Before mating, the great crested grebes perform a spectacular courting display. Head-shaking, diving, fluffing out the plumage and presenting each other with water plants while rearing out of the water, breast to breast, make up an extraordinary ballet.

Dragonflies

SIX LEGS AND FOUR WINGS

Depending on the species, their body is long and thin or short and flat, and is often brightly coloured green and black, red, brown or blue. They all have three pairs of legs and two pairs of wings.

They are grouped into two main divisions: Zygoptera, the damselflies, have wings that are held up one against the other when the insect is at rest and their flight is weak and fluttering; Anisoptera, the true dragonflies, rest with their wings outstretched at right angles to their body and their flight is swift and powerful.

The eyes are two enormous half-globes at the front of the head. In fact, each eye is composed of thousands of small units that together create a mosaic picture like the image on a computer's visual display screen. Dragonflies are very sensitive to movement and pinpoint their prey with their eyes. They flee at the slightest sign of danger.

EXTRAORDINARY AIRCRAFT

The shape and the way in which their wings are joined to the thorax, together with the various possible angles of wingbeat, allow dragonflies to fly very fast. Some can reach a speed of twenty-five kilometres an hour. They are also acrobatic flyers and can hover and even fly backwards. On the other hand they cannot walk.

A VERY SHORT LIFE

The adult dragonfly lives only a few days or weeks, just long enough to find a mate and breed. By the waterside two blue dragonflies have paired up and seem to be performing a strange ballet. Their mating position sometimes takes the shape of a heart, sometimes a V and at other times, as they fly in tandem, a funny little train.

The dragonflies' eggs, several hundred of them per batch, are laid very close to or totally under water. Other insects, birds and fish devour large quantities of them. The rest hatch into larvae, which live in water.

One or two years later, after several moults, the new adult dragonfly will take to the wing to start its short life in the air.

A VORACIOUS CARNIVORE

In a pond, you can catch dragonfly and damselfly larvae with a net. If the larvae are broad and flat they belong to the Anisoptera. If they are long with a little feathery tip, the gills, at the end of the abdomen, they are Zygoptera larvae.

If you place the larvae in an aquarium or similar large glass container filled with pond water and a few waterweeds, you will be able to observe them easily. Do not place the aquarium in direct sunlight, though, as everything in it will die.

Throw a small earthworm or a tadpole into the water. The larvae will be attracted by its movements. Quick as a flash, one of them shoots out its long, pincer-like lower lip that until this moment was folded under its head. The lip is known as the mask. The larva uses it to seize the worm or tadpole and to draw it back to its jaw. The larva then consumes its meal at leisure resting on the sandy bottom of the aquarium or hiding in the weeds to feed.

Do not, at any cost, put a dragonfly or

The mating ballet.

Dragonflies and damselflies often fall prey to birds.

The end of the metamorphosis of a dragonfly.

damselfly larva in the aquarium where your goldfish live as you would run the risk of your fish being eaten.

IT'S HARD TO BECOME ADULT

After moulting for the last time, the larva will get out of the water by clinging to the stalk of an aquatic plant. The skin on its head will split, then the skin on its back, just as if an invisible zip-fastener was opening.

Getting out of this armour requires a lot of effort. The larva will need several hours to change into the perfect insect, which must then spread its wings and dry itself in the sun. An adult dragonfly or damselfly will then appear, brand new and brightly coloured.

In July or August, when inspecting the edges of a pond it is not difficult to find the dried-up skin cases of old larvae. They are usually attached to plant stems, a few centimetres above the surface of the water.

DRAGONFLIES AND DAMSELFLIES UNDER THREAT

It is rare to find dragonflies or damselflies in dry areas; the insects do well only in damp conditions.

The drying out or pollution of ponds, streams and lakes deprives them of their feeding and breeding grounds and leads to a gradual decrease in the size of their populations.

These are astonishing insects, masters in the art of elegance and speed. Their beauty inspired naturalists to give them such poetic names. Perhaps on one of your walks by a pond you will see the brightly coloured large red damselfly, the emperor dragonfly and the red-eyed damselfly.

The Coot

AN UNGAINLY BIRD

Far more numerous than ducks or moorhens, the coot is the most common aquatic bird in Europe. It is a rather clumsy-looking bird that swims slowly and has a laborious take-off which involves first taxiing on the surface of the water. But you must not be deceived by appearances: the coot is not as clumsy as it seems.

The size of a small duck but with a more rounded body, the coot is slate-grey to black all over. On its head there is a slightly darker hood. Its white beak and curious white hairless shield on its forehead allow you to identify it without hesitation; the shield has given rise to the expression 'bald as a coot'. Its greenish feet bear lobed toes that end in long claws. Male and female are identical.

ON LARGE EXPANSES OF WATER

Ponds, lakes or broad rivers – coots can be found on any expanse of water provided it is large enough and has reeds, rushes and bushes along the banks. The birds use the reeds and rushes to make their nests at the water's edge.

Essentially herbivorous, coots occasionally supplement their diet with small fish, tadpoles or insect larvae. Sometimes they even feed on the eggs or chicks of other species.

The two annual broods of six to nine yellowish, brown-speckled eggs hatch into nidifugous chicks, that is newborn birds that are able to swim away from the nest barely a few hours after they have broken out of the shell. The chicks are able to fly and fend for themsleves after eight weeks.

DIVING AND TAKING-OFF

Let us follow a coot. It swims slowly and each kick of the legs is accompanied by a nodding of the head.

Suddenly it lifts its head up as if wanting to fly off. But on the contrary, it dives towards the bottom of the pond. The coot is a champion diver and is able to make good use of its legs and wings to move about under water. It disappears for a little while; just how long depends on the time it takes to pluck a clump of grass from the bottom. It brings the grass to the surface in its beak and proceeds to eat it.

LONG-DISTANCE FLYING AND GETTING ABOUT ON LAND

From time to time, one of the coots on the pond leaves the group and flies off. Although it appears to have difficulty taking off, once airborne the coot flies fast and steadily. It is capable of remarkable flying feats. In a ringing experiment, a coot ringed and released in northern Germany turned up a day and a half later in France on the Channel coast, a distance of 730 kilometres.

The coot is rather clumsy on land, flopping its feet down as it walks. At the slightest sign of danger it dashes into the water where it feels more secure. As soon as it feels threatened it dives underwater and slowly comes back up to hide under a lily pad with only its beak and eyes out of the water. From this position it surveys its surroundings without being seen as long as is necessary.

If winter becomes too harsh and the surface of the pond freezes over, coots fly off to spend a few days on neighbouring

A carefully concealed hide allows you to birdwatch without being seen.

A few hours after they hatch out the young coots are able to leave the nest.

A cousin of the coot, the moorhen moves as easily on land as on the water.

rivers that remain free from ice until their usual home returns to normal.

WATCHING WITHOUT DISTURBING

In winter, coots gather together and go and search for food as a group. This is the time of year when they are easiest to approach. In the stillness of a winter's day you will need to gently and quietly clear a path through the reeds to get close to the edge of the pond.

To watch the birds without being seen, it is a good idea to build a hide on the bank of the pond. Having cleared a path to the water's edge, remove any stems, twigs and leaves that might be noisy to walk on from a small patch of flat ground. Then push a few stakes into the earth and fix them in place. Cover the structure with canvas or tarpaulin. Make a small opening in the front of the hide through which you can observe the birds with binoculars. After a few days all the animals in the area will be used to this contraption and will go about their lives as if you were not there.

A COUSIN: THE MOORHEN

Dark brown and grey and sometimes almost black, like the coot, the moorhen differs from its cousin by its slightly smaller size, its red beak and forehead, the white line on its side, and its white undertail.

More discreet than the coot, the moorhen avoids large gatherings and lives on small expanses of water, usually under the cover of aquatic plants. It can live on ponds and lakes in town parks. It spends less time on the water and can often be seen on land, particularly in meadows, where its long toes leave remarkably large tracks.

The Edible Frog

A LEGENDARY ANIMAL

A native of western and central Europe, this amphibian was introduced from the Continent in the 19th century. Its colour varies from green to brown. It has a light-coloured stripe along the centre of its back, a brown stripe on either side, and large, irregular, often squarish, black spots all over its top surface. The white underparts are sometimes speckled with black.

Its front legs each have four toes. The hind legs, which when fully extended are as long as the rest of the body, each end in five toes that are joined one to the other by a supple membrane; the feet are said to be webbed.

Its mouth, widely gaping up to its ears, contains a tongue that is folded lengthways in half. To capture its prey the frog shoots its tongue out at great speed then pulls it back into its mouth. Spending most of its time in water, the edible frog dives at the slightest sign of danger, then comes back up to the surface with only its nostrils and large protruding eyes emerging.

Like all amphibians, the edible frog presents peculiarities that make it a legendary animal. Its body takes on different shapes as the animal develops from egg into adult: the frog is said to undergo metamorphosis.

GROWING UP

From the egg the tadpole emerges and this lives in water and breathes through gills. When it hatches, it has no legs but does possess a tail. The adult frog, which breathes through lungs, can come out onto land. It has two pairs of legs but has lost its tail.

The metamorphosis: from the egg to the adult frog.

1. frogspawn
2. the tadpole with its gills
3. the gills disappear
4. the hind legs grow
5. the front legs appear
6. the tail shrinks, then disappears

You can breed tadpoles in an aquarium or glass container. In May collect a batch of eggs, or spawn, which you will find attached to plants at the bottom of a pond. A single female lays between 5000 and 10000 eggs. Collect some pond water as well for the eggs will die if you use tap water in the aquarium. Put the aquarium in a sunny position but out of direct sunlight.

After they have hatched, the young tadpoles should be fed with thin slices of raw potato or small pieces of cooked lettuce. Choose an aquarium or glass container which is broader than it is deep to make oxygenation of the water easier. Place in the bottom a few flat stones arranged so that they are only partly covered by the water; the frogs will then be able to come out onto 'dry land'. Also, put wiremesh on top of the aquarium as even when they are small frogs can jump several centimetres high.

As adults, in one leap they can cover distances of more than a metre.

After three to five months a tadpole turns into a frog, which then comes out of the water. It will return only to breed As a young frog it measures about two centimetres. It will be fully grown about three years later and will then measure about eight centimetres in length.

Never forget that animals do not like living in captivity and that they should be taken back to the place from where they were collected as soon as possible.

TO EAT OR TO BE EATEN

The edible frog feeds on small animals: flies, caterpillars, spiders, small snails, slugs. In water, it will eat fish eggs or very young fish.

Its predators are equally numerous: it is part of the diet of herons, storks, rats, pikes, grass snakes, foxes, otters…and

The frog falls victim to many predators: birds, mammals, fish or snakes.

The frog suddenly shoots out its sticky tongue on which its prey gets stuck.

people some of whom catch it to eat the flesh on its legs. The tadpoles are a choice food item for the voracious larvae of the dragonfly and the diving beetle.

HIBERNATION

Like all 'cold-blooded' animals, – that is those which cannot keep their body temperature constant – the frogs change their way of life as winter draws near.

At the end of October, as soon as it gets cold, frogs disappear from sight. They hide among stones or in the mud along the banks of ponds and, as the temperature of their body falls below a certain level, they enter into a lethargic state. When fishermen drain ponds to clear them of weeds and leaves they sometimes find hundreds of kilos of frogs lying motionless in the mud.

CRIES IN THE NIGHT

Frogs croak. At night, their cries are not always well-received in the neighbourhood of the pond. History books tell us that in medieval times peasants had to beat the ground around the moats of castles throughout the night to keep the frogs quiet while their masters slept.

FROGS AND WEATHER-FORECASTING

The frogs' cries and their emerging from ponds in the spring are linked to popular beliefs about the weather.

But what they announce is often contradictory. Their croaks indifferently signal rain or fine weather. Popular sayings include "If frogs sing at night it is a sign of bad weather" and "The frog's croaking heard at nightfall announces good weather."

The Pike

BUILT FOR SPEED

Shaped like a torpedo, the pike has a long body and its fins are set far back. These characteristics coupled with a very supple backbone allow it to reach amazing speeds over short distances in the water: in one second it can cover a distance equal to ten times its length.

Its back is greenish, its sides have lighter spots and its underside is white or yellowish. Its head has a flat snout and a wide mouth with strong jaws that bristle with backward-slanting teeth. Caught in such a trap, its prey cannot escape. This can have fatal results for the pike, though, as it cannot get rid of large prey jammed in its throat and will choke on it.

The pike's sight is poor; its eyes, perched high on either side of its head, allow it only limited vision. On the other hand, it receives information about movements in the water through a system of pit organs, which are sensitive microphone-like structures situated on its lower jaw and gills. These pick up sounds in the water.

WILL EVERY LITTLE PIKE REACH ADULTHOOD?

In spring, in the shallow water of ditches or flooded meadows, the female pike lays several tens of thousands of eggs. Many are eaten by other fish. The ones that hatch produce a small larva that clings to water plants. After a few days the larva becomes a jack, a young pike. This quickly has to start its carnivorous life by catching its own food. It also has to continually escape predators. The parents take no care of their eggs or young.

The pike lays thousands of eggs. Only a few will reach the adult stage.

AN ENORMOUS APPETITE

The pike is often accused of consuming its own weight in fish each day. This is an exaggeration. But this fresh-water 'shark' is indeed a formidable carnivore. When it is hungry it fills up its stomach completely then digests the food slowly, sometimes taking several days to consume it all. In the meantime, it does not hunt.

The pike will eat almost anything. While its diet consists mainly of fish, it will also eat frogs and occasionally a duckling or a young bird fallen from the nest. It even has no hesitation in attacking another pike. It has been known for two pikes to choke to death when trying to eat one another.

The size of its prey is impressive. A seventy-two-centimetre-long pike recently caught in a net had in its stomach, partly digested, another pike that measured forty-three centimetres in length, more than half its own size.

Its voracious appetite is such that sometimes when we catch an old pike we find several hooks caught in its jaws, memories of struggles with other fishermen who had to give up their lines when they broke under the strain of trying to land such a big fish.

AN EFFICIENT HUNTER

The pike stalks its prey. Hidden among grasses, it waits motionless for a fish to swim within reach. Then it plunges forward to catch it. Its mediocre swimming performance over long distances force it to look for prey that are easy to capture: fish that are ill, malformed or wounded. In this respect the pike is very useful: it limits the spread of diseases among fish and the increase in numbers of undesirable fish. It performs the same role in water as the fox in woods and forests.

Three types of spoons for pike-fishing.

LOOKING FOR THE PIKE

Early one morning in autumn go to the edge of a pond where you know there are pike, and try and catch one.

Should you try your luck with cast fishing, use a large 'spoon', an artificial bait that will spin round in the water at the end of the line. You will need to entice the pike out of its hiding place so cast your line near the edge of the clumps of grass. But beware of getting your line entangled in the waterlilies. The pike, keen to catch prey moving within its reach, might pounce and grab the bait with the side of its jaws. You must then strike immediately and try to reel it in.

If you choose to experiment with live bait, you must use the largest roach you can find and attach it to a hook on a steel line. The pike will be interested but wary of the trap, which will move back and forth in front of its nose. First it will sniff the bait, then come a little way out of its hiding place to nibble at it. Suddenly, your float bobs up and down. Woe betide you if you get impatient and strike too soon! You must wait, experienced fishermen say, for as long as it takes to chew a piece of gum until all the flavour has gone!

The pike has finally made up its mind. It bites the bait to kill it, then swallows it. There is a violent tug on your line. Now you need to work on the hooked fish and tire it out. The struggle can sometimes last half an hour.

What a moving and proud moment it is when you have managed to catch in your net a magnificent fish that has fought so bravely!

You need a lot of patience and know-how to catch a pike in your net.

The Stickleback

THE CAT-CHOKER!

The stickleback is both a commonplace and original fish.

It is commonplace as it can be found almost anywhere in calm waters, from slow-flowing rivers to still ponds. It is a pretty little fish with a blue-black or sometimes olive-green back, bronze-coloured sides and a silvery belly. Its skin is very smooth since it has no scales but the animal is covered along the sides with a few bony plates that constitute a sort of armour.

The stickleback is original in that it bears on its back and along its flanks very sharp spines which it raises when angry or feels there is danger ahead. These spines have given rise to its common name of stickleback and the nickname of cat-choker; the spines irritate the cat's throat and it tries to cough up its meal, but the fish gets stuck and the cat chokes.

The stickleback feeds on worms, small crustaceans, insect larvae, fish eggs and young fish.

This small fish can undertake long migrations and live not only in fresh water but also in sea-water near coasts.

A NEST-BUILDING FISH

From April to June, at the beginning of the breeding season, the male becomes more brightly coloured. Its throat and belly turn a brilliant red and the fish is then called a red-throat. It takes over a territory and drives out other male sticklebacks. In the centre of the territory it builds a nest of small pieces of plant debris, lodged among the stems of water plants in fresh water and of seaweeds in the sea.

THE STICKLEBACK'S NEST

Spring has arrived. The male puts on its multicoloured outfit. Here it is rubbing itself on the bottom of the aquarium in endless contortions. It is getting rid of the mucus that comes out in large quantities from a hole near its anus. This sticky transparent string upsets the stickleback's balance in the water. The fish tries to get rid of it by sticking it to a stone or plant as we would do with a piece of Sellotape stuck to our fingers. This secretion glues mud and the plant debris together and allows the male progressively to build a small tunnel.

The continuous process of secreting mucus and enlarging the tunnel goes on for two or three days until the nest is complete.

AN ATTENTIVE FATHER

The male's movements and colour attract a female, which lays a few hundred eggs in the nest. The male entices other females to do the same so that eventually the nest may contain several thousand eggs. The eggs incubate for one to four weeks depending on the temperature of the water – the warmer the water the faster they hatch.

The male stands guard, motionless, in front of the nest and protects it against attacks. It keeps an eye on the eggs until they hatch.

Experiments have shown that introducing into the aquarium a model fish that is painted red just like the male will trigger the male stickleback's aggressive reaction towards a competitor for females.

On the other hand, you might see a

Nest-building and egg-laying.

40

good 'father' fish driven by hunger to eat the eggs or the young fry.

THE CAPTURE

The stickleback can be caught with very basic fishing equipment; just a simple rod, line and hook will do. Very often, even if the hook is small the stickleback will remain attached on the maggot or the piece of worm without having swallowed it as its mouth is rather small. Its teeth are not dangerous but they can, however, cut the line if it is very fine.

If you want to keep sticklebacks in an aquarium, check that those you have collected have not been wounded by the hook. A wound can rapidly become infected and this will kill the fish.

The stickleback is not an especially delicate animal but still you must take a few precautions when handling it. Do not hold it too tight or you may injure it or perhaps hurt yourself on its spines. The best way is to hold the stickleback's head between your thumb and forefinger, closing its gills with a gentle pressure.

When you have taken the fish off the hook, put it in a bucket of water. But don't keep it in the bucket for too long nor in too great a quantity of water as it requires a constant fresh supply of oxygen to stay alive. Having got the stickleback home safely, transfer it to your aquarium with similar care.

If your aquarium is big enough and has an aerator and a filter, if the temperature and acidity level of the water are suitable, you can keep the sticklebacks in your home for a long time. You might see them build a nest, which is a fascinating process but difficult to observe in nature.

The Crayfish

A KNIGHT IN ARMOUR

Just like lobsters, crawfish, crabs and prawns, its cousins that live in the sea, the crayfish has a body covered with a shell made of chalk and other calcium compounds which protects it against the attacks of its enemies. It is on account of this shell that all these animals are called crustaceans, which means covered with a sort of crust.

Mainly greenish or reddy-brown, the crayfish hides under stones or among the roots of aquatic plants near the banks of rivers or lakes. Its discreet appearance and essentially nocturnal habits mean it escapes inquisitive eyes.

The crayfish has two pairs of antennae and eyes that are borne on the ends of stalks. It also has five pairs of legs, which are thin and jointed 'and attached to the underside of the thorax.

The first of these pairs is larger and more highly developed than the others and ends in large powerful pincers.

The abdomen is made up of segments that are joined one to another and allow up-and-down movement. The last of these segments is shaped like a five-bladed fan and acts as a tail fin.

ACTION AND REACTION

On gently lifting a stone along the river bank you have discovered a crayfish. Slowly it crawls away across the river bed, seems to hesitate, then goes round an obstacle, all the time keeping low and flat against the bottom of the river. Its only wish is to escape.

If you try to catch it, the crayfish disappears in a cloud of churned up muddy or sandy water. At the slightest hint of danger it swiftly flicks its abdomen and fan-shaped tail downwards and forwards. This sudden action of pushing hard against the water and forcing it forwards, makes the animal shoot backwards in exactly the opposite direction. It is the same reaction principle by which a jet engine forces out a gust of air to push an aircraft forwards. Should you manage to catch a crayfish, hold it still in the water using two fingers placed on either side of its thorax. The animal will carry on flicking its abdomen and tail in this manner in an effort to try and free itself.

The crayfish hunts at night, crawling along the bottom of the river or pond with its large front legs outstretched. It uses its antennae and its eyes to locate its prey, which it then catches with its pincers. If you use a magnifying glass, you will see the tiny 'teeth' on the 'jaws' of these tools. Its diet includes snails, tadpoles and insect larvae.

As the crayfish grows, its shell becomes too small. It then abandons the old shell and makes a new one. This is the process of moulting. Like all crustaceans, the crayfish has to repeat this process several times during its life.

A VICTIM OF GREEDINESS

The river crayfish has had an unhappy fate. People like the delicate flavour of its flesh. It is a gourmet dish of the highest order.

Fished from rivers in great quantities, the crayfish has not been able to breed quickly enough to keep up its numbers and has almost disappeared completely from many waterways. In addition, early this century an epidemic spread rapidly through crayfish populations in many parts of Europe and wiped out whole communities of this animal.

The female crayfish carries its eggs for about 6 months attached to its abdomen.

When it hatches, the young crayfish measures less than a centimetre.

44

Each crayfish needs its own hole: under a stone, in a brick...

Rather rashly, a North American species of crayfish was introduced in Germany to try and re-stock rivers in Europe. This species was more resistant to the illness and to pollution than the native European crayfish. It also hunted during the day not at night, and bred faster. However, it was smaller and its flesh was not quite so tasty. The North American crayfish became established in Germany and moved into most European waterways. It is mostly this species that is fished nowadays. Of course, it is now considered to be undesirable as it prevents the European crayfish from re-establishing itself in its former homes.

A STEADILY DECLINING ENVIRONMENT

The crayfish is a relatively demanding animal. When it moults, for a time it is without its 'armour' and is vulnerable to predators so it must live along banks that will afford it hiding places. Also, breathing through gills, it requires very pure water.

The straightening of rivers and the removal of aquatic plants and tree stumps along the bank that restrict the flow of water mean that the cracks in which the crayfish needs to hide during moulting and where it shelters in witner to hibernate are no longer present.

Pollution of water is now affecting rivers and streams not only in and around urban areas but also in the countryside. There is, however, a ray of hope for the crayfish. Water-purifying works play an important part in improving the quality of the water: in areas where the rivers have been cleaned up, the crayfish is making a comeback.

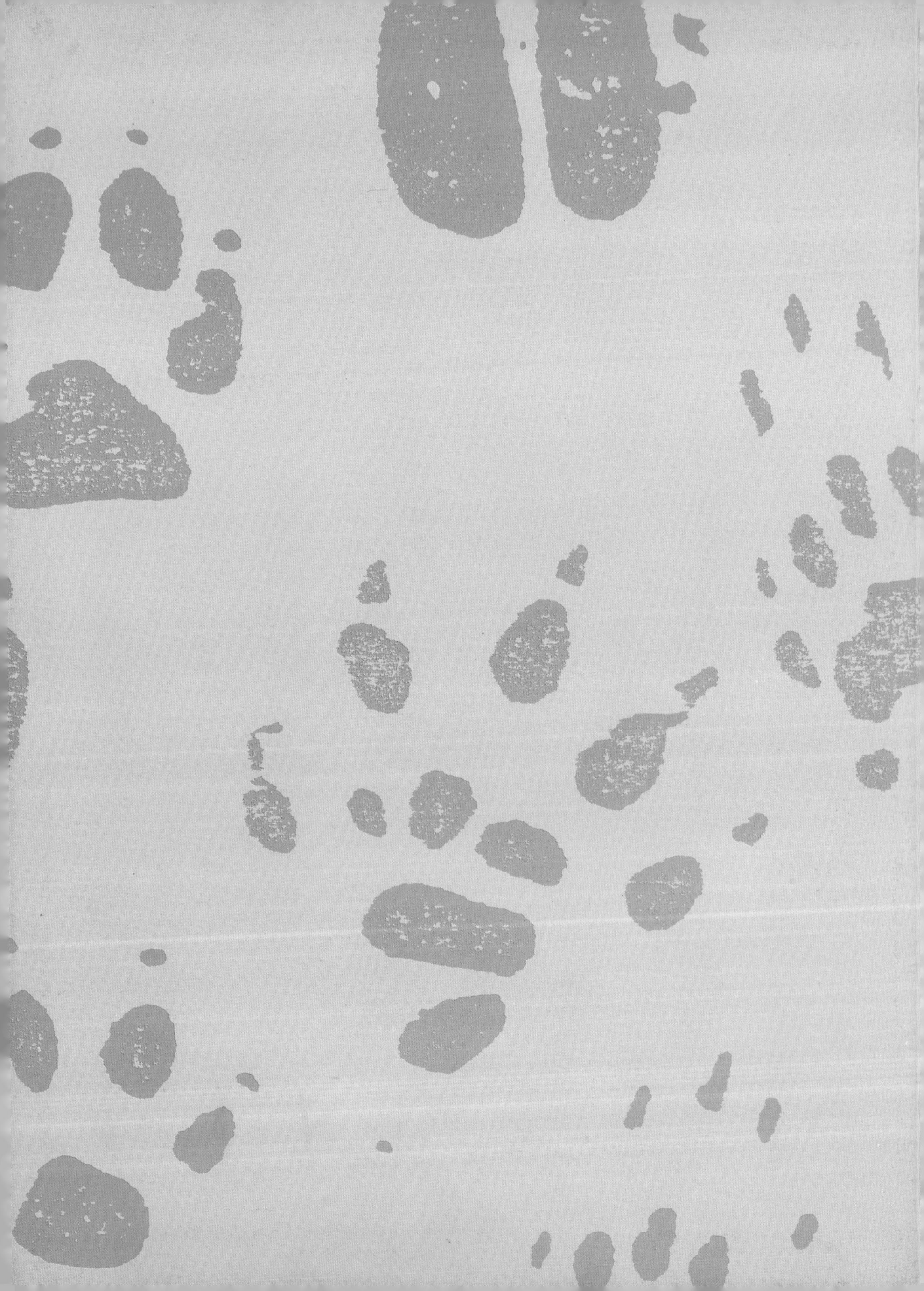